COWBOY

IRENE FRANCK &
DAVID BROWNSTONE

GROLIER
EDUCATIONAL

Credits and Acknowledgments

abbreviations: t (top), b (bottom), l (left), r (right), c (center)

Image credits: Granger Collection: 5t, 8, 10, 13t, 22, 24, 25b, 26t; Liaison Agency, Inc.: 23l (Michael Gallacher), 25t (Dave Nagel), 28t (M. Crawford Samuelson); Library of Congress: 4t, 9, 26c, 26b, 27b; National Archives, Environmental Protection Agency, Documerica Project: 13b (David Hiser), 19t; National Geographic Society: 5b, 6, 7tr, 14, 19b, and 27t (William Albert Allard); Photo-Disc: 2 and 3 (Jack Hollingsworth); Photo Researchers, Inc.: 11 (R. Rowan); 29t (James Amos); The Stock Market: 1 (Terry Eggers); 7b, 12, 18, and 23r (D. R. Stoecklein); 15; 20 (Dale O'Dell).

Original image (4b) drawn for this book by Lizbeth Nauta of Nauta Design.

Photos for projects (16, 17, and 21) taken for this book by Bill Touchberry of Touchberry Media.

Project consultant: Peggy Franck Sargent
Photo researchers: Robin Sand and Susan Hormuth
Copy editor: Michael Burke
Book design: Combined Publishing

Our thanks to the above people and sources, and also to Joe Hollander, Phil Friedman, and Elizabeth Ricci at Grolier Educational; and to the librarians throughout the northeastern library network, in particular to the staff of the Chappaqua Library—director Mark Hasskarl; the expert reference staff, including Martha Alcott, Maryann Eaton, Carolyn Jones, Jane Peyraud, Paula Peyraud, Carolyn Reznick, and Michele Snyder; and the circulation staff, headed by Marilyn Coleman—for fulfilling our wide-ranging research needs.

Library of Congress Cataloging-in-Publication Data

Franck, Irene M.
　　Dress through the ages / Irene Franck & David Brownstone
　　　　p. cm.
　　Includes bibliographical references and indexes.
　　　　Contents: v. 1. Deep-sea diver – v. 2. Clown – v. 3. Astronaut –
　　v. 4. Ballerina – v. 5. Cowboy – v. 6. Knight – v. 7. Roman soldier – v. 8. Samurai –
　　v. 9. Baseball player – v. 10. Traditional Guatemalan – v. 11. Pirate –
　　v. 12. Egyptian princess – v. 13. Surgeon – v. 14. Bedouin – v. 15. Pilgrim –
　　v. 16. Renaissance lady.
　　　　ISBN 0-7172-9558-3 (set: alk. paper) – ISBN 0-7172-9550-8 (v. 1 : alk. paper) –
　　ISBN 0-7172-9554-0 (v. 2 : alk. paper) – ISBN 0-7172-9546-X (v. 3 : alk. paper) –
　　ISBN 0-7172-9551-6 (v. 4 : alk. paper) – ISBN 0-7172-9543-5 (v. 5 : alk. paper) –
　　ISBN 0-7172-9544-3 (v. 6 : alk. paper) – ISBN 0-7172-9541-9 (v. 7 : alk. paper) –
　　ISBN 0-7172-9553-2 (v. 8 : alk. paper) – ISBN 0-7172-9547-8 (v. 9 : alk. paper) –
　　ISBN 0-7172-9556-7 (v. 10 : alk. paper) – ISBN 0-7172-9548-6 (v. 11 : alk. paper) –
　　ISBN 0-7172-9542-7 (v. 12 : alk. paper) – ISBN 0-7172-9555-9 (v. 13 : alk. paper) –
　　ISBN 0-7172-9545-1 (v. 14 : alk. paper) – ISBN 0-7172-9552-4 (v. 15 : alk. paper) –
　　ISBN 0-7172-9549-4 (v. 16 : alk. paper)
　　　　1. Costume–History–Juvenile literature. 2. Clothing and dress–History–Juvenile literature. 3. Dress accessories–History–Juvenile literature. [1. Costume.]
　　I. Brownstone, David M. II. Title.

　　GT518 .--F73 2001
　　391–dc21   00-047603

Contents

Cowboys

Cowboys spent much of their lives on the range. From an 1886 book called *A Texas Cow Boy*, this picture of life in a "cow camp" shows cowboys of the day herding cattle in the distance, while the cooks prepared them a meal at the chuck wagon (lower left).

American cowboys (and "cowgirls," too) were the riders and cattleherders of the Old West. They worked out-of-doors, in all weathers, on the huge Great Plains, from Texas all the way to Montana. They worked hard and long, in bitter northern winters and scorching desert summers, in the saddle all day, and through brushfires, tornadoes, floods, and stampedes. Their greatest days started when the West was opened after the Civil War ended in 1865, and they lasted into the early 1900s. Cowboys still work on the ranches of the West, often on horses, though now also with jeeps and trucks to help them.

There are Canadian cowboys, too, who work on the part of the Great Plains that stretches from the Canadian border north almost to the Arctic Circle.

South of the United States–Mexican border, Span-ish-speaking cowboys have

Cowboys drove herds of cattle hundreds of miles to the nearest railroad, for shipping to markets in the East. These cowboys were driving Texas longhorns through the streets of Dodge City, Kansas, in 1878.

ridden herd on cattle all the way to Argentina, deep in South America. There and in Uruguay they are called *gauchos*. In other parts of South America, cowboys are usually known as *huascos* and *llaneros*.

The earliest cowboys of the American West were the Mexican cowboys called *vaqueros*. Mostly of combined Spanish and Native American ancestry, these vaqueros herded cattle on the great ranches of what was then northern Mexico. The ranches were known as *haciendas* in Spanish, and the ranch owners were called *charros*.

Many vaqueros became Mexican-Americans after the United States took much of northern Mexico in the 1840s, during the Texas War of Independence and the Mexican War. Before then Texas, the whole American Southwest, and California had been part of Mexico. Vaqueros were then joined on the plains by English-speaking cowboys from the United States. In California, cowboys were sometimes called *buckaroos*, an English version of *vaqueros*. After the Civil War, many African-Americans, often former slaves, also became cowboys.

Whatever their countries and backgrounds, cowboy looks, cowboy clothes, and cowboy gear all came directly from what cowboys do as the riders and cattle-herders of the great western plains.

Cowboys go by many names. This is a South American *gaucho* from Argentina. He wears a blanket on his shoulder, in the regional style. Otherwise his outfit is much like those worn in North America.

Cowboy Clothes

Cowboys work in all kinds of weather. This modern cowboy, wearing a yellow slicker, is herding cattle in a snowstorm near Bearcreek, Montana.

Some kinds of cowboy clothes are fairly standard outdoor all-weather working clothes. Among these are warm wool shirts and pants, along with long flannel underwear, all aimed at protecting cowboys from the cold. From 1850 on, many cowboys replaced their woolen pants with "Levis," heavy cotton pants with metal rivets. These were first made by immigrant tailor Levi Strauss for miners in California's Gold Rush and then became popular throughout the West. Today they are known as "blue jeans" and are worn all over the world.

The cowboy's vest, with many pockets, is another very useful piece of clothing, as is the cowboy's oiled, often-yellow slicker, worn in wet weather. In the deep northern winter, cowboys have always worn the kinds of heavy, often fur-lined hats, coats, and gloves worn by other men and women working outdoors.

Cowboys also wear some very special clothes and gear. Among these are the kinds of big "ten-gallon hats" and riding boots that we usually think of when we say that someone "looks like a cow-

A shirt with a fancy design and a leather belt with a beautifully worked buckle are also standard cowboy gear, like those worn by this young cowboy, along with his jeans and high-crowned hat.

The bridle helps a rider control the horse. It includes the harness over the horse's head, the metal *bit* in the horse's mouth, and the leather strips called *reins* held in the rider's hands. Pushing the boots deep into the *stirrups*, as this cowgirl is doing, helps the rider stay in the saddle. So does the high back (*cantle*) on the saddle, which makes long hours of riding more comfortable.

boy." Bandannas, gloves, gauntlets, and chaps also all have important uses for working cowboys. All of these are discussed later on in this book.

Spanish Names

Spanish-speaking vaqueros were the first cowboys. Because of that, they named many of the basic clothes and tools used by American cowboys. Later, as American ranchers and cowboys flooded into the West, many of the Spanish names were shortened or changed over time to fit into English. That's how the cowboy rope, in Spanish called *la reata* or *lazo*, became the *lariat* or *lasso* (see "Working Tools," on page 22). Leather leggings named *chaparerras* in Spanish became the cowboy's *chaps* (see "Special Gear," on page 12). In the same way, *calabozo*, the Spanish word for *jail*, became the *calaboose*.

This is a Spanish-speaking California vaquero in 1852, shortly after the United States took the region from Mexico.

For their special needs as the riders and cattleherders of the plains, cowboys wear spurs on their boots. They must also have the right kinds of saddles and other riding equipment. For handling cattle and working out on the range, cowboys need to be very skilled with lariats (ropes), working from their range-wise horses. Many cowboys also wear and use guns for several purposes, though most cowboys— even in the days of the "Wild West"—were very far from being any kind of gunmen.

Cowboy clothes and gear came directly from their need to work outside in all kinds of weather, in the saddle all day and sleeping rough out on the range many nights. Like the Bedouin desert dwellers of the Sahara, and the Eskimo peoples of the Arctic, cowboys need to dress in layers, winter and summer, in the hot southwestern desert and in the icy northern winters. That's the way to hold on to your body fluids and protect the body from extremes of heat and cold.

Opposite is a picture of a working cowboy. Every piece of clothing and gear he's wearing has an important purpose in the cowboy's work. However, some cowboy clothes, especially hats and boots, can also become "showpieces," highly prized for their quality and style.

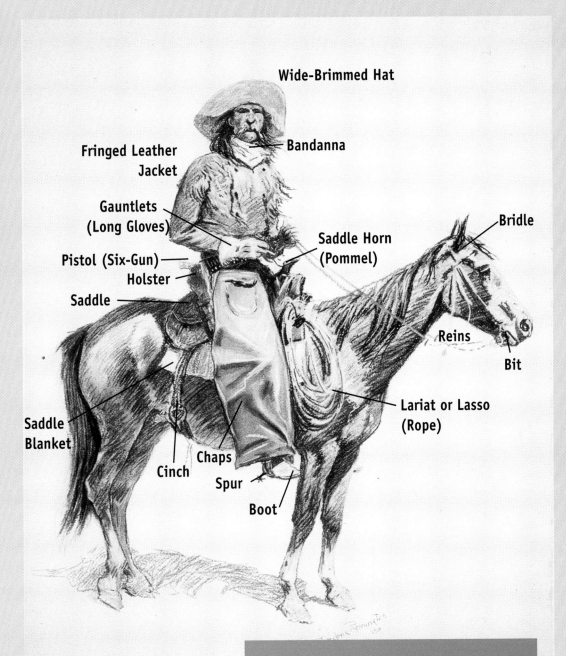

Wide-Brimmed Hat

Bandanna

Fringed Leather Jacket

Gauntlets (Long Gloves)

Saddle Horn (Pommel)

Pistol (Six-Gun)

Holster

Saddle

Bridle

Reins

Bit

Saddle Blanket

Lariat or Lasso (Rope)

Chaps

Cinch

Spur

Boot

This Arizona cowboy was drawn by noted western artist Frederic Remington and first published in *A Bunch of Buckskins* in 1901. The picture shows much of the main clothing and gear associated with cowboys.

9

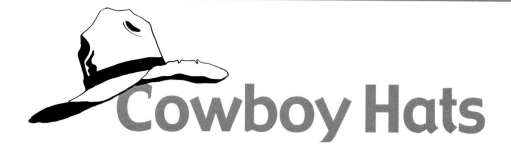

Cowboy Hats

The vaqueros and later cowboys of the hot southwestern desert needed hats that would shade their faces, heads, and necks from the burning sun. Their hats also had to hold in some cooler air on top of their heads, and to keep out the rain, so they could see. All those things were done by the *sombrero* (shade provider), the earliest of the cowboy hats. Its high crown holds a layer of cooler air on top of the head, while its broad brim provides shade and keeps water

Like most cowboy hats, sombreros could be plain or fancy. These are clearly the fancy kind, worn by two Mexican cowboys from Buffalo Bill Cody's Wild West Show in around 1900.

out of the eyes. In cold weather, however, the high crown helps keep the head warm. A chin strap or thong keeps the hat on the head, even when the cowboy is on a galloping horse.

In time the sombrero would become the cowboy hat, often called a "Stetson," after the leading manufacturer of cowboy hats. High-crowned and broad-brimmed, the Stetson was often called a "ten-gallon" hat, because the company claimed its hats were so waterproof that your horse could drink out of it. They put a trademark picture of a horse doing just that on every one of their millions of hats.

Stetsons and other good cowboy hats were made of animal furs, mostly rabbit and beaver, pressed into high quality, water-resistant felt. Poorer quality cowboy hats were often made of wool pressed into felt. The use of beaver in all kinds of hats led to the near-extinction of beaver by the early 20th century.

At work or rest, as here on a Montana ranch, cowboys are seldom seen outdoors without their hats.

Chaps come in all shapes, sizes, designs, and colors, as shown by this group of Arizona cowgirls. They are generally held up by a belt or tied straps.

Special Gear

*E*very working cowboy expects to live with dust, often in great clouds. It may be the choking dust kicked up by a Montana trail herd on a bitterly cold and windy day. Or the swirls of red dust blowing out of West Texas on a hot summer day. Or even a sudden sandstorm out in the southwestern desert. A broad-brimmed hat helps; but what helps most is a big, usually brightly colored cotton neckerchief called a *bandanna*. The name most probably comes from the Spanish word *banda* (ribbon) or the Portuguese word *bandana*. You can pull the bandanna up over your face, pull down your hat, and protect your face, eyes, and neck from the stinging, blinding dust that is part of a cowboy's daily life.

Cowboys also need to protect their hands, wrists, and lower arms from several kinds of dangers. Without such protection, cowboys could very easily suffer deep rope burns or severe cuts from such haz-

rds as barbed wire, cactus, horns, and animal bites. Heavy leather gloves provide the protection cowboys need. Some prefer a short style of leather glove, worn with separate heavy leather cuffs. Others prefer longer one-piece leather gloves called *gauntlets*.

Cowboys also need to protect their legs from various dangers. To do so, Mexican vaqueros developed *chaparerras* or *chaparejos*. These were heavy, very strong leggings or "overpants," worn on top of regular pants and held up by a belt or tied straps. The name comes from

Cowboy gear could get very fancy indeed, like that worn by Buffalo Bill Cody in this 1910 poster advertising his "positively last appearance" in his famous Wild West Show.

This young cowboy was being fitted for chaps in a Colorado leather shop in 1972.

Shaggy chaps called woolies and a bandanna around his neck help keep this young Nevada cowboy warm, along with the campfire in front of him. Behind him are tents used by cowboys sleeping out on the range.

notable danger they guarded against: the thornbush thickets called *chaparral*, which can rip and tear at a cowboy's unprotected legs.

Early *chaparerras* were usually made of goatskin. Later English-speaking cowboys in the American West generally made theirs out of heavy cowhide leather. They also shortened the name *chaparerras* to *chaps*, often spoken as if the word were spelled *shaps*.

The two basic kinds of American chaps are *shotgun chaps* and *batwing chaps*. The names come from the way they look on a cowboy's legs, having nothing to do with either shotguns or bats. Shotgun chaps fit tightly around a cowboy's legs—so tightly that the covered legs look a lot like the barrels of a double-barreled shotgun. (For an example, see the second cowgirl from the left in the photograph on page 12.) Batwing chaps are larger, looser, and fastened at the side of a cowboy's legs, making them more comfort-

This African-American cowboy is wearing beautifully designed leather cuffs, along with fancy batwing chaps.

able to wear. These chaps flare out widely from the cowboy's leg, looking something like the wings of a bat—the source of the name. Some Mexican vaqueros and American cowboys wear shorter chaps, ending just below the knee, called *armitas* (see pages 2 and 3).

For the deep cold of the northern plains, most cowboys wore *woolies* (see page 14). These are chaps of any style with the fronts made of warm buffalo hair, angora goat hair, or furs.

Chaps

What You Need

a pair of jeans or other pants that fit you
a belt that fits you
2 yards of leather-colored felt fabric (36-inch width)
one or two large sheets of newspaper
a yardstick
a pair of sharp, fabric-cutting scissors
a pair of paper-cutting scissors
a package of self-stick Velcro dots or strips
a pencil
a package of straight pins
thick white craft glue (optional)
tape (optional; any type)
buttons, needle, and thread (optional)

How to Make "Chaps" for a Costume

1. Spread your jeans out flat on a table or the floor. Using your yardstick, measure the length of the leg from the waist to the bottom of one leg. Write down and save this measurement.
2. Measure the width of the leg from the outside seam to the inside seam. **Add six inches to that measurement.** Write down the result and save it.
3. Measure the length of your jeans from the waist to where the legs begin (under the zipper, if there is one). Write down and save this measurement.
4. Open up a large sheet of newspaper, and lay it out smoothly on a table or the floor. If your jeans are longer than the newspaper, tape two sheets together.
5. To start making a paper pattern for your chaps, you will draw a rectangle (a "stretched-out" box) on your sheet of newspaper. Using your pencil and yardstick, mark off the leg length of your jeans (the measurement from Step 1). Then mark off the leg width (the **final result** from Step 2). Use these measurements to draw your rectangle (see photograph below), using the yardstick to help you draw straight lines.

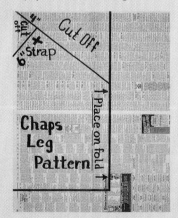

6. Starting from the **right-hand top corner** of your rectangle, mark off where the leg would begin, under the zipper area (the measurement from Step 3). Using your yardstick as a guide, draw a line from this mark to the **top left corner** of your rectangle. The result will be a large triangle shape (see photograph at Step 5).
7. On the side of the rectangle below the mark you made in Step 6, write "Place on the fold" (see photograph at Step 5).
8. On the **left side** of your rectangle, measure down six inches and make a mark.
9. On the line you drew in Step 6, measure four inches from the top left end and make a mark.
10. Using your yardstick as a guide, connect the two marks you made in Steps 8 and 9. The result will be a small triangle with one end cut off (see photograph at Step 5).
11. Using your paper-cutting scissors, cut out the paper pattern you just drew—that is, cut out the rectangle, and then cut off the large and small triangles. The result should look like the paper pattern in the photograph at Step 13.

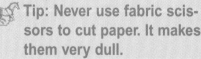 **Tip: Never use fabric scissors to cut paper. It makes them very dull.**

12. Fold your felt in half, the long way. Lay it out on a hard, smooth table or on the floor (not on a carpet or rug). Smooth out as many wrinkles and ridges as you can.
13. Place your paper pattern (from Step 11) on top of the folded felt (see photograph at right). **Make sure that the**

side you marked "Place on the fold" is on the fold. When you are sure the pattern is in the right place, pin it down.

14. With your fabric-cutting scissors, cut the felt along the pattern. Do not cut on the edge along the fold. This uncut fold of felt will wrap around your inner leg (see photograph on the bottom of page 13). Unpin your pattern, and set it aside. The result is your first chaps leg. Save your felt scraps.

15. Repeat Steps 13 and 14 to make the other chaps leg. Remember: Do not cut on the fold.

16. Using felt scraps (from Steps 14 and 15), measure and cut four strips, about one inch wide and six inches long. These will become loops to hold up your chaps.

17. Take one chaps leg (from Step 14) and two felt strips (from Step 16). Make loops of the strips, and pin the ends to each of the two "pointed" areas on the top part of the chaps leg. (The photograph at Step 23 shows how the loops fit onto the chaps legs.) Repeat for the other chaps leg.

18. Put your belt through the four loops you just made, and try your chaps on for size, over your jeans. You may need to adjust the length of the loops. If your chaps are too long, you can cut pieces off the loops and repin them. If the chaps are too short, you can add pieces to the loops (just staple them onto the original loops).

19. Once you are comfortable with the fit, take the chaps off. Staple the loops to the chaps legs, and take the pins out.

20. Now to hold the outer edges of the chaps together, you'll put Velcro dots on the insides of the chaps. Smooth out one chaps leg (folded as when you cut it out), and see where you want to place the Velcro dots. They should be about an inch from the outer edge. A good rule of thumb is to use three dots (see photograph at Step 23 for placement), but if your legs are long, you can use four or five dots. Use your pencil to mark where you want the dots to go.

21. Stick Velcro dots onto the spots you just marked.

Tip: Velcro comes in two forms: smooth and rough. You must have one of each to match up and fasten. You'll place one kind of dot on the front inside of each chaps leg, and the other kind on the back inside.

22. Put your chaps on again. See if the Velcro dots meet in the right places, and if the chaps are comfortable. Move the dots, if necessary. Once you're satisfied with the fit of the chaps, take them off, and staple the dots into place.

23. To cover the staples (from Steps 19 and 23), you can use your scraps in a creative way. In the photograph below, we have used scraps as "buttons" and fringe, with stars for extra decoration. You can also use another color fabric, actual buttons, appliqués, or other kinds of decoration. These can be sewn on, glued, stapled, or stuck on with Velcro. Use your imagination! If you use glue, wait for it to dry before wearing your new "chaps."

Tip: Save any leftover felt scraps. You can use them for decoration in your "spurs" project (on page 21).

Cowboy boots come in many different designs and colors, as shown on this row of cowboys.

Boots and Spurs

*R*eal cowboy boots are riding boots, not walking boots. That's why they are so very uncomfortable for walking, with their high inward-pointing heels, tight ankles, narrow toes, high stiff tops, and thin soles. Most modern "cowboy boots" are made to look like old-time cowboy boots, but are actually made much more for comfortable walking than for riding. They have lower and straighter heels, wider ankles, wider toes, medium-sized tops, and often much thicker, softer soles.

The early English-speaking cowboys of the American West started with ordinary boots, made for all-purpose outside work, but not for riding. Mexican vaqueros, however, had long since developed the right kinds of boots, made for cowboys who worked in the saddle all day. Everything that made their boots uncomfortable for walking made them right for riding.

High inward-pointing heels (many four inches high) were made to fit into stirrups (see "Working Tools," on page 22). With high heels, the cowboys' feet did not slip out of the stirrups, as they fought their way on horseback through chaparral, roped fast-moving cattle, and did all the other highly skilled jobs in the cowboy's trade. These heels made the boots

Unlike traditional high-heeled cowboy boots, the boots worn by this Texas ranch hand are very plain and flat-heeled.

This view of a Montana rodeo cowboy from below shows the thin and worn sole of his boots, the high "stacked" heels, the spurs sticking out, and the chaps protecting his legs.

terrible to walk in. Try it some time, and you'll see why!

Tight ankles made boots hard to get on and off, and could even make walking painful. But they also protected cowboys' ankles and feet from dust, water, thorns, stones, and other objects that could easily get in through loosely fitted boot tops.

Narrow toes slid much more easily into stirrups than did wider and rounder or box-toed boots. Thin soles were uncomfortable for walking, but they helped riders to control their stirrups and therefore their horses.

High boot tops (some as much as 18 inches high) covered cowboys' lower legs, offering extra protection against thorn bushes, cactus, and cuts, adding to that offered by chaps (see "Special Gear," on page 12). Some cowboys prefer to wear high boots with short chaps.

With their high tops and narrow ankles, cowboy boots were very hard to get on. That's why most were made with pulling straps called "mule ears," because that's what they looked like (see drawing above).

Cowboy boots also soon became highly prized fancy-dress clothes, just like many cowboy hats. Even though most early cowboys were paid very little (often only $20 to $30 a month), many had their boots custom-made by bootmakers. They might spend as much as a month's pay on a good pair of leather boots, often with a lot of fine handcrafting and fancy stitching.

Over their boots, cowboys generally wore *spurs*, in Spanish called *espuelas*. These are small metal wheels or spikes that are strapped around the ankle and stick out at the back of the boot heel. Spurs come in many different styles,

Hanging off the spur on this cowboy's boot are jinglebobs, named for their jingling sound when in motion.

but all serve the same purpose: to help the cowboy control a horse, by prodding its sides to get more speed or to change direction.

Some early Mexican and American spurs had very sharp points that were used brutally, often even drawing blood. However, these became less and less common as time went by. In the great days of the American cowboy, very few riders would deliberately use their spurs to hurt their horses. Those who did

were condemned by other cowboys and by ranchers. To make sure that they could not even accidentally hurt their horses, many cowboys filed down the spiked rowels on the ends of their spurs.

Many spurs had small dangling bits of metal attached. Called *jinglebobs*, these served no useful purpose, but many cowboys wore them because they liked the jingling sound they made.

Spurs

What You Need

a pair of shoes or sneakers that fit you

a package of black elastic, $\frac{1}{2}$ inch wide

a stapler

measuring tape or a piece of string, 1 foot long

a yardstick or ruler

scissors

Self-stick Velcro dots or pieces of Velcro tape

pins or paper clips

for decorations: buttons, iron-on appliqués, large metal washers, felt scraps (optional)

How to Make "Spurs" for a Costume

1. Put on your shoes. With the measuring tape or string, measure the distance around your foot at the arch—that is, from the top of the arch (where a bow is, if the shoes tie), under the instep (in front of the shoe heel), and back to the top. Write down this measurement, or mark it on the string.

2. Cut two strips of black elastic, each the length of the measurement from Step 1.

3. Take one of the elastic strips, and make a large loop, so the ends slightly overlap. Staple the overlapping ends together twice.

Then slip the loop over the middle of your shoe. Repeat with the other elastic strip.

4. With the measuring tape or string, measure the distance around your foot at the heel—that is, from where the elastic lies on the instep (in front of the shoe heel), to the back of the shoe heel, and around to the elastic on the other side of your shoe. Add three inches to that measurement, and write down the result.

5. Cut two strips of elastic, each the length of the final measurement from Step 4.

6. Take one of the strips from Step 5, and loop one end of it around the elastic on one side of a shoe (see photograph at Step 12). Use a pin or paper clip to hold the new loop in place. Then slip the old elastic loop off your shoe, and staple the new, small loop twice.

7. Loop the free end of the strip from Step 6 around the other side of the old elastic loop. Staple the ends of the new, small loop together twice.

8. Slip the old elastic loop back onto your shoe, so the new, larger loop is at your heel. This new loop will be very loose.

9. Pinch together the loose part of the elastic loop behind your heel. Use a pin or paper clip to hold the pinched elastic together.

Tip: Don't pinch the loop too tightly, or your "spurs" will be uncomfortable.

10. Take the elastic strips off your shoe. Staple the pinched elastic together twice. This is where you will place the decoration or "jangly" pieces of your spurs.

11. Do Steps 6–10 for the other shoe.

12. Now for decorating! In the photograph here, we have used iron-on appliqués, stuck with Velcro to the "pinched" section of elastic sticking out

behind the shoe heel. However, you can use many more things, a few of which are listed above. They can be sewn on, glued on, stapled on, or stuck on with Velcro. Use your imagination! If you want to make "spurs that jingle-jangle-jingle," you can use some large metal washers. Experiment to see how to fasten them, so they will jingle when you walk like a cowboy! If you use glue, wait for it to dry before you wear your new "spurs."

Tip: You can use scraps from your "chaps" project (on pages 16–17) for decorations here.

13. Once you're finished decorating, slip the original elastic loops over your shoes, with the decorations at your heel. Enjoy your spurs!

Working Tools

Charles M. Russell's 1904 painting *The Bolter* shows a cowboy about to drop a running noose around the head of a runaway bull—a difficult and dangerous job, taking a great deal of skill.

*T*he *lariat*, or *lasso*, is one of the cowboy's most important working tools. This is a long rope with a loop at the end, called a *running noose*, which is used to catch such animals as cattle and horses. In the original Spanish, the names were *la reata* (the rope) and *lazo* (snare), a kind of trap (see "Spanish Names," on page 8). Later cowboys mostly called lariats "ropes" and described their work with them as "roping." The most common American cowboy ropes were 40 to 60 feet long.

For a cowboy, skill at roping was almost as important as riding skill. Cowboys used ropes to catch unbranded cattle and hold them for branding with the ranch's ownership mark. Cowboys also used ropes for controlling cattle in roundups and on cattle drives, for catching wild horses, and for a good many other purposes. Roping exhibitions and contests also became very popular in Wild West

The saddle was and is one of a cowboy's most prized possessions. Though often beautifully detailed, it is a working tool. This saddle has tape wrapped around the saddle horn, so it will hold a rope better.

Out on the range, extra supplies, food, and cooking gear are often carried by wagon, as on this Texas ranch. Cowboys also carry extra gear in saddle bags and saddle rolls, as behind the saddle of this cowboy in the foreground.

shows, rodeos (see page 26), and even on the stage.

The saddle was another key tool. Working cowboys were strong, steady, highly skilled riders, who spent more time every day in the saddle than doing anything else. There were several different kinds of saddles, but all served basic working cowboy needs. All had strong wooden frames, covered by heavy leather, with deep, sturdy seats. All had a high saddle horn (*pommel*) at the top front of the saddle. This was handy for holding a coiled rope; it was also used to brace the rope, horse, and rider against the power of a running bull or wild horse (bronco). All had high backs (*cantles*), making them comfortable and secure for cowboys, who moved and twisted into many positions as they did their jobs. All had leather bands (*cinches*) around the horse, to hold the saddle firmly in place. And all had strong, deep *stirrups*, loops hanging down from either side of a saddle, into which riders put their boots (see "Boots and Spurs," on page 18).

Along with the saddle went the horse's bridle, bit, and reins, all used to help the rider control the horse (see photograph on page 9). Under the saddle went a saddle blanket, to protect the horse from irritation and sores that might otherwise be caused by the saddle.

Cowboy Guns

Most cowboys in the Old West carried one or more guns as part of their working equipment. Most carried a long gun—either a rifle or a shorter, lighter carbine. Carbines were favored by many cowboys because, although less accurate than rifles, they were much better suited to use by riders.

Many cowboys also carried a smaller weapon—a pistol or another kind of side arm. Called *handguns*, because they could be used with one hand, these were usually worn in holsters belted around the waist. However, they were sometimes carried in a pocket to reduce weight.

Although cowboys are often pictured in films as gunmen, nothing could be further from the truth. Cowboys some-

African-American cowboy Nat Love, better known as Deadwood Dick, is pictured here with his rifle and his saddle. This photograph was taken in the late 19th century and then painted in oils.

times shot poisonous snakes and threatening animals, but they did not generally use their guns to shoot other cowboys. Cowboys worked together, needed each other, and protected each other. There were certainly outlaws and peace officers who used their guns on people, and occasional cowboys who got in trouble, but the image of cowboys as gunmen is false.

One of the most popular guns used by American cowboys was the 15-shot 1873 Winchester repeating rifle, which shot a .44 caliber bul-

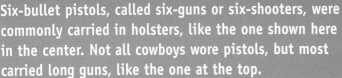

Six-bullet pistols, called six-guns or six-shooters, were commonly carried in holsters, like the one shown here in the center. Not all cowboys wore pistols, but most carried long guns, like the one at the top.

let. Among handguns, one of the most popular was the six-shot 1873 Colt Peacemaker, which shot a .45 caliber bullet. This was the famous "six-gun" or "six-shooter" of the Old West, used by cowboys, outlaws, and law officers alike.

Annie Oakley

Among the many outstanding women of the Old West, one of the most famous was Ohio-born sharpshooter Annie Oakley (1860–1926), whose birth name was Phoebe Anne Moses. A natural crack shot, she defeated well-known sharpshooter Frank Butler in a shooting match in 1875. They married in 1876, and then worked together as a sharpshooting team.

Annie Oakley joined Buffalo Bill Cody's Wild West Show as a sharpshooter in 1885, and toured with the show for 16 years, with her husband as her manager. She became a worldwide superstar during her years with Buffalo Bill. Sioux chief Sitting Bull, who also joined the show in 1885, nicknamed her "Little Sure Shot," and called her his adopted daughter. Little, indeed—the great sharpshooter weighed less than 100 pounds and was under 5 feet tall!

Rodeo

Early rodeos featured cowboys of widely varied backgrounds, including Mexican and Native American cowboys, as shown on this poster (right) for Buffalo Bill Cody's Wild West Show, printed for a 1905 tour of France.

Many early professional rodeos were for men only, but women were a major attraction in rodeo events at other places, as at this state fair in the 1940s.

African-American cowboy Bill Pickett became famous for inventing the rodeo event called bull-dogging or steer wrestling—so famous that he starred in his own movie, *The Bull-Dogger,* as shown in this poster.

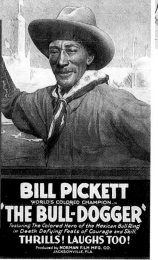

A rodeo is part Wild West Show, part circus, and mostly a series of events that test and show cowboy skills. It didn't start that way. For Mexican vaqueros, the earliest cowboys, *rodeo* was simply the Spanish word for roundup. After cattle round-

In some rodeo events, as here in bull riding, the rider can only hold on with one hand, keeping the other one raised in the air, like this cowboy at a rodeo in Alberta, Canada.

Women were part of many early "wild west" shows, as seen in this advertisement for Pawnee Bill's Historic Wild West Show.

ups, with cowboys all gathered in one place, they began to compete in events that tested their skills, such as in horse riding, bull riding, and roping. The result was the modern rodeo. By the 1880s, rodeos were awarding cash prizes to winners. A standard series of rodeo events began to develop, along with ever-increasing audiences and competitions.

Wild West Shows also became very popular, and these had a lot of "rodeo" features. Buffalo Bill (William F.) Cody began touring with his first Wild West Show in 1883. It was soon a worldwide hit, with stars such as Annie Oakley

(see page 25), Sioux chief Sitting Bull, cowboys Johnny Baker and Antonio Esquivel, and many other highly skilled cowboy riders, ropers, and sharpshooters.

Annie Oakley was far from alone. From the first, there were many women in rodeos and Wild West Shows, as there are today. However, women had a hard time making their way in the professional rodeo world after the 1920s, coming forward again strongly only in the 1990s.

PAWNEE BILL'S HISTORIC WILD WEST
AMERICA'S NATIONAL ENTERTAINMENT

BEAUTIFUL DARING WESTERN GIRLS AND MEXICAN SEÑORITAS IN A CONTEST OF EQUINE SKILL.

There are five main, recognized events in rodeo:

Bulldogging (steer wrestling) was invented in the early 1880s by African-American Texas cowboy Bill (Willie M.) Pickett. He would jump off his horse and run beside a cow or bull, which was kept running in a straight line by someone riding on the other side. Pickett would then bite the upper lip of the bull, drawing its head to one side. At the same time, he would slow the bull down by pulling backward, grip the bull's head and twist it to the opposite side, and force the bull down to the ground. Today cowboys no longer bite the bull's lip. Bulldogging required great strength and skill, and became a major rodeo event. Like many other cowboys, Pickett was injured many times, though he continued to bulldog until the 1920s. Bulldogging, like some other rodeo events, has often been criticized as harmful to the animals involved.

Bareback bronc riding involves a rider and a bronco—a wholly "unbroken" (untamed) bucking horse. The rider holds on

Girls and boys have their own rodeo competitions. This teenage cowgirl is twirling her lariat at a Little Britches rodeo in Colorado.

to a leather harness (with one hand only), and wears boots and spurs, but has no saddle, reins, or other means of controlling the horse. The rider must stay on for at least eight seconds.

Saddle bronc riding also pits a rider against a bucking bronco. The rider has a light saddle, stirrups, and a piece of rope to hold with only one hand. A rider who touches anything with the other hand or whose foot leaves a stirrup is ruled disqualified, scoring no points. All points, up to 100, have to be scored in just eight seconds.

Bull riding is an extremely dangerous event, in which the rider tries to stay on a bucking, often spinning bull, holding on with only one hand to a rope that goes around the bull's body. Here, too, the rider must stay on for at least eight seconds.

Calf roping involves a cowboy on horseback following the calf into the open arena and casting a rope around its neck. Then, as fast as possible, the rider jumps off the horse and ties three of the calf's legs together, passing the rope around the legs twice and ending with a half-hitch knot around two legs. Meanwhile, the cowboy's horse holds the original rope tight around the calf's neck.

Many people strongly criticize calf roping as brutal, because many calves are hurt and some killed by broken

necks when they are originally roped and pulled down. The same criticism applies to steer roping, an unofficial and often-banned rodeo event, in which the cowboy's running horse pulls the original rope tight around the steer's neck, pulling it to the ground and sometimes breaking its neck.

Women riders developed another rodeo event: *barrel racing*. They demonstrate skill, speed, and control by riding their horses through a course marked by barrels.

Words to Know

bandanna A large, often brightly colored neckerchief worn by cowboys to protect their faces, necks, and eyes out on the range.

bareback bronc riding A *rodeo* event, in which a rider has to stay on a bucking *bronco* for at least eight seconds.

barrel racing A *rodeo* event, largely developed by women, which involves riding a horse through a course marked by barrels.

branding The burning of a rancher's ownership mark into the hide of a cow, bull, or other animal.

bridle A harness around a horse's head used by a rider to control the horse. It includes the metal *bit* in the horse's mouth and the *reins*, long leather straps attached to each end of the bit, with the free ends in the rider's hands.

bronco A wild horse, wholly or largely untamed.

bulldogging (steer wrestling) A *rodeo* event, invented by Bill Pickett, in which a cowboy stops a running bull and wrestles it to the ground.

bull riding A *rodeo* event, in which a rider has to stay on a bucking bull for at least eight seconds.

calf roping A *rodeo* event, in which a rider has to rope and then, on foot, tie the legs of a calf as fast as possible.

chaparral Dense stands of thornbushes, sagebrush, and small trees that working cowboys often ride through while out on the range.

chaps Heavy leather leggings worn over regular pants to protect their legs, originally called *chaparerras* or *chaparejos*. Chaps with fronts made of hair or fur are called *woolies*. Tight-fitting chaps are called *shotgun chaps*, while those that flare out at the sides are called *batwing chaps*. Knee-length chaps are called *armitas*.

gauntlets Heavy leather gloves with long cuffs that protect cowboys' hands, wrists, and lower arms.

jinglebobs Small metal attachments to *spurs* that make jingling noises as cowboys walk or ride.

lariat (lasso) A 40- to 60-foot rope with a loop (*running noose*) at one end, used by cowboys for many purposes. From the Spanish *la reata* and *lazo*.

Levis Durable cotton work pants made with metal rivets instead of buttons, worn by cowboys, miners, and other workers. Developed in 1850 by immigrant tailor Levi Strauss, they became internationally popular as *blue jeans*.

mule ears Pulling straps at the tops of cowboy boots, to help get them on, so named because they look like the ears of a mule.

rodeo Western show with events that test several cowboy skills, among them *barrel racing*, *bulldogging*, *bareback bronc riding*, *saddle bronc riding*, *bull riding*, and *calf roping*.

saddle A leather-covered riding seat on the back of a horse or other animal. Sticking up at the front is a *saddle horn* (*pommel*), used to hold ropes and for bracing a rope, as against a bull pulling against a horse and cowboy. The raised rear part (*cantle*) makes the saddle comfortable for long hours of riding. The saddle is held in place by a leather band (*cinch*) around the horse.

saddle bronc riding A *rodeo* event, in which a rider has eight seconds to score points by showing control of a lightly saddled *bronco*.

sharpshooter A highly skilled, often prize-winning shooter, such as Annie Oakley. Also widely used to describe any very good shooter.

six-gun (six-shooter) A kind of pistol widely used in the West, which shot six bullets. The most popular model was the 1873 Colt *Peacemaker*.

sombrero Wide-brimmed, high-crowned Mexican hat, worn by early Mexican cowboys (*vaqueros*) and ranchers (*charros*).

spurs Small metal wheels or spikes, sometimes with *jinglebobs*, strapped to the backs of cowboy boots. Cowboys poke the spurs into the sides of horses to control their movement.

stampede A quick, out-of-control, often very dangerous charge by a herd of cattle or other large animals.

Stetson The name of a leading manufacturer of American cowboy hats. *Ten-gallon hats* are often called "Stetsons."

stirrups Leather loops that hang off the sides of a *saddle*. They help a rider to get on or off a horse, and to control the horse in motion.

ten-gallon hat A nickname for a high-crowned American cowboy hat. The *Stetson* company claimed that its hats were so waterproof that your horse could drink out of one, sparking the nickname.

vaqueros Early Mexican cowboys, who were the first cowboys of the American West.

On the Internet

The Internet has many interesting sites about cowboys and their gear and culture. The site addresses often change, so the best way to find current addresses is to go to a search site, such as **www.yahoo.com**. Type in a word or phrase, such as "cowboy" or "rodeo."

As this book was being written, several museums of western life had websites containing information about cowboys:

http://www.cowboyhalloffame.org/
The Cowboy Hall of Fame and Western Heritage Center, which contains a "virtual tour" of the museum, with images and information about its displays.

http://www.autry-museum.org/
The Autry Museum of Western Heritage, founded by movie star and singing cowboy Gene Autry. It contains images from its galleries and information about its research center and projects.

Other special-interest sites on cowboys include:

http://www.cowboypal.com/
CowboyPal, special-intersest Home of the Silver Screen Cowboy, one of several sites devoted to film cowboys.

http://www.africancowboys.com/
Africans in the Diaspora, the Black Cowboys, a site that focuses on African-American cowboys, with images and information about notable figures.

http://www.cowgirl.net/
The National Cowgirl Museum and Hall of Fame, which focuses on the role of women in the West and in rodeos.

Books about Cowboys

Your local bookstore and library will have many books on cowboys. This is just a sampling of them.

Armitage, Susan, and Elizabeth Jameson. *The Women's West*. Norman: University of Oklahoma Press, 1987.

Beard, Tyler. *100 Years of Western Wear*. Salt Lake City: Peregrine Smith Books, 1993.

Cusic, Don. *Cowboys and the Wild West*. New York: Facts on File, 1994.

Dary, David. *Cowboy Culture*. New York: Avon, 1982.

Durham, Philip, and Everett L. Jones. *The Negro Cowboys*. Lincoln: University of Nebraska Press, 1983.

Erickson, John R. *The Modern Cowboy*. Lincoln: University of Nebraska Press, 1981.

Havinghurst, Walter. *Annie Oakley of the Old West*. Lincoln: University of Nebraska Press, 1992.

Jordan, Teresa. *Cowgirls: Women of the American West*. New York: Anchor Books, 1982.

Kalman, Bobbie. *Bandannas, Chaps, and Ten-Gallon Hats*. New York: Crabtree Publishing, 1999.

Katz, William Loren. *Black People Who Made the Old West*. New York: Crowell, 1977.

Kauffman, Sandra. *The Cowboy Catalog*. New York: Crown, 1980.

McCracken, Harold. *The American Cowboy*. Garden City, NY: Doubleday, 1973.

Murdoch, David. *Cowboy*. New York: Knopf, 1996.

Slatta, Richard W. *The Cowboy Encyclopedia*. New York: Norton, 1996.

_____. *Cowboys of the Americas*. New Haven: Yale University Press, 1990.

Taylor, Lonn, and Ingrid Maar. *The American Cowboy*. New York: Harper and Row, 1983.

Index